CHOOSING TO BE A SWAN

CONNIE BENSLEY

CHOOSING
TO BE A SWAN

BLOODAXE BOOKS

ISBN: 1 85224 314 7

First published 1994 by
Bloodaxe Books Ltd,
P.O. Box 1SN,
Newcastle upon Tyne NE99 1SN.

Bloodaxe Books Ltd acknowledges
the financial assistance of Northern Arts.

Cover printing by J. Thomson Colour Printers Ltd, Glasgow.

Printed in Great Britain by
Cromwell Press Ltd, Broughton Gifford, Melksham, Wiltshire.

for Paul and Guy

Acknowledgements

Acknowledgements are due to the editors of the following publications in which some of these poems first appeared: *Aquarius, The Chatto Book of Cats* (Chatto & Windus, 1993), *The Guardian, The Independent, London Magazine, Navis, The Observer, The Observer Arvon Poetry Collection* (Observer Books, 1994), *Outposts, Poetry Book Society Anthology 3* (PBS/Hutchinson, 1992), *Poetry Review, Poetry with an Edge* (Bloodaxe Books, new edition, 1993), *Seam 1, Sixty Women Poets* (Bloodaxe Books, 1993), *Smith's Knoll, Spectator, Sunk Island Review* and *The Times Literary Supplement.*

'Wheel Fever' was a prizewinner in the 1993 Arvon International Poetry Competition.

Contents

Molluscular Romance

The octopus has many arms –
   I'd like to know if you
   wish I had too.

The octopus turns white when shocked
   and I'd turn white and grieve
   if you should leave.

The octopus has got three hearts
   but I had only one
   and now have none.

Choosing To Be a Swan...

was not one of my best moves −
the balancing so tricky, the flapping
so draughty, the little loosened
feathers getting up her nose so that

she sneezed and shuddered
when stillness could have been helpful
and lay exhausted when shuddering
would have been acceptable.

When she laid the egg, her husband
was all rolling eyes and ironical looks,
but sensibly kept his mouth shut.
I twisted thunderbolts between my fingers,

but let him live on. The egg
will hatch forth a boy and a beautiful
peaceful daughter called Helen.
What more could a cuckold ask for?

Cars

Beside the railway lines
cars are waiting – metal pets
parked in abutting flocks
cooled by absence: witnesses
to strife, aggrandisement, love
adultery, death.

They die too. In car graveyards
they lie jumbled, piled
like animals awkwardly mating,
waiting to be transmuted,
crushed to metallic essence,
finally overtaken.

Wheel Fever
May 1877

Frank Reynolds has ordered a *Coventry*,
48 inches high and with all
the new improvements.

But it cost £14, and I am afraid
to sink so much money – it would be almost
three months of my salary.

All the fellows in the village
have bicycle fever, and none
more than myself.

* * *

Rode on Aubrey's wooden cycle
into Warboys, to see a Spider-Wheel
which Monty has for sale.

But the tyres were tied on
with pieces of twine, so I did not
part with my cash.

* * *

I've done it! I could not bear to wait
any longer. I now possess a *Coventry*
(without the new improvements).

Before I paid, I took it for a spin
but lost the treadle,
landed in a heap

and had to have it taken back
in the cart, and put together.
But after that

I rode off round the lanes
as right as twelve o'clock.
and pleased as Punch.

* * *

Coming back from a spin today, I met
Mr Dodds with his cartload of bread.
He must have known

that horses shy at bicycles, but
he did not get down, and sure enough
his wretched animal

reared, backed into the dyke, and emptied
22 stone of bread and 6 stone of flour
into the water.

* * *

Set out with James Black, to ride
to the prayer meeting, but
by Redman's corner

he ran into me, knocked me off,
broke my handle, bent my treadle, and fell
on top of me.

* * *

I am receiving unpleasant letters from
Mr Dodds. I do not believe that flour
can be so dear.

Unlike Aubrey or Frank Reynolds,
I can now ride my bicycle
with arms folded.

* * *

I was riding my bicycle with my arms
folded on my way to Doddington,
when I hit a stone

and pitched on my head. Managed to get up
and stagger on, covered with blood
and feeling faint.

Of course I could not help Uncle
in the shop. The carrier put his pony in
and took me home.

* * *

Could not move this morning, so stiff
and sore. My bicycle will take three days
to put right.

I miss it dreadfully. Frank Reynolds
does not seem keen on the idea
of lending me his.

But I have had a carrot poultice put on
my eye and I shall soon be fit enough
to ride again.

Surprised on a Train

Five strangers are sleeping here:
so close, I could touch them
so close, they could touch me.

By the time I caught the train
they were neatly stacked above
muffled and inert in the darkness.

Shelved, we hurtle forward
hour after hour. Which
is the stentorian breather?

At last, the first light draws
a rectangle round the door.
A foot dangles down beside me:

it is large, blunt, tanned.
On the instant, I extrapolate
burliness, machismo, chest curls;

but it is followed down
by a small, dishevelled lady
with a faded floral sponge-bag.

Checkout

Like the chameleon
I had one eye on you at first:

you, obviously planning
to eat alone; choosing

the modest chicken breast; squeezing
the smallest avocado.

My swivelling eye steadied,
narrowed, measured.

Secretly, I loosened my tongue.

Personal Column

Married man would like to meet
girl, affectionate, petite,
for afternoon diversion.

Vicar sighs. He'd like to meet
married man. It's wrong to cheat:
he hopes for a conversion.

Jane writes off from school to meet
married man. He sounds so sweet
she longs for the excursion.

Blackmailer would like to meet
married man, to make discreet
enquiries re perversion.

Now his wife would like to meet
man – her eyes are cold as sleet –
she writes: I am a blonde, petite,
and spoiling for diversion.

The Covetous Cat

Because the common is remote
they walk along hand in hand.

On the path ahead of them
some bird-lover has scattered bread

and in the middle of it a plump cat crouches
chewing at the crusts.

Cats don't really like bread, the man remarks
he only wants it because it's someone else's.

Like you, she thinks,
withdrawing her hand slightly.

Jump

They were given the bedroom
with the three dolls' houses.

She thought that he, being an analyst,
would involve her in symbolic play,

moving the doll figures about:
Why have you put the child in the attic?

*Why is the mother doll lying
under the table?* – that sort of thing.

Not at all. He simply kicked off his shoes,
flopped on his bed and went to sleep.

She pulled out the doll from under the table
and put her on the windowsill.

Jump! she whispered, *It's your big chance.*

Politeness

They walked awkwardly along the towpath
bumping together, because his arm
was round her shoulder. He was saying:
I shall always remember this walk.
I'll never forget last night.
I'll never forget you. Oh God.

After a pause, she made a short
non-committal noise. The morning had turned
wet and dark. She felt dilapidated by the rain
and of course had forgotten her umbrella
due to the unexpected turn of events.
Trust me, he said, *you will, won't you?*

Trust him to what, she wondered.
Which men could one trust? Any man
carrying a musical instrument, perhaps?
Any man walking along reading a book?
Most doctors – with reservations about those
wearing bow ties. *Trust you to what?* she asked.

To never let you down, he said,
splitting the infinitive, crushing her
against his wet tweeds. She fought
for breath as he loomed over her.
Little one, I can't let you go.
I'll be back on Thursday. Expect me.

So many imperatives. The situation
had become unwieldy. She longed
for buttered toast, looked furtively
at her watch. *I know, I know, we have*
so little time. The suffocating squeeze
into the spongy lapels.

I've never felt like this before.
Have you ever felt like this before?
Fatigue and embarrassment were
all too familiar to her. She stirred the leaves
with the toe of her boot. *No*, she said
politely. *Not exactly like this.*

In the Conservatory

Though we spring apart,
my earring, caught in your beard,
winks indiscreetly.

Prey

Outside, in the cherry tree
a wood pigeon is trampolining –
grey wings outspread – trying to catch
the shiny fruit.

On the windowsill the black cat
quivers and bristles. His covetous eye
is green as glass, his teeth ache to crunch
feather and bone.

The tiny drama takes you to the window.
Don't move. I'm just getting the feel
of the shading at your throat: the siren curve
of your mouth.

A Brief Marriage

The park keeper lifted
our honeymoon blanket: *There are rules
to be observed. But everything's
in order here, so far as I can see.*

I was married to you for one night
and then I woke up. Fortunately
I'd kept the receipt, the small-print guarantee.

I settled myself back for sleep.
The biscuit, the camomile tea.

Near dawn, the pillow cooled,
the gulled heart slowed
but sleep's sweet rhythms were askew for me.

Although I'd only married for the night
the whole day passed before I struggled free.

Chemistry

The doctor told him:
These tablets may have side-effects.

That night the dreams started:
reaching from his past
like a chain of beacons flaring,
signalling in the dark
across hilltops, seas, marshy places,
purple, scarlet and lustrous –
scenarios more bizarre and erotic
than anything invented in his youth.

Each night he awoke repeatedly
rumpled, sweating, smiling.

Repeat prescriptions changed hands:

Mitte one tab. nocte, 1001 nights.

Egged on by Passion –

he attired himself in terylene,
scraped his fingernails
with the grapefruit knife, plucked
the strings of his hair across
his scalp and realigned them
at the mirror until it was so late
that he had to run to confront her.

As usual, she was preoccupied –
locking up the library
and fishing in her bag for some
lost object, so failed
to notice him, or to hear
his tentative murmur, or
the faint drumming of his head
on the municipal wall behind her.

Angela on My Mind

Outside my window pane, the sky is blue.
I know I should get up and start the day –
I cannot move, I'm thinking about you.

I phone my office, say I have the flu:
they claim they haven't noticed I'm away.
Outside my window pane, the sky is blue.

Why did you leave me for that awful Hugh?
as I recall, you told me he was gay.
I cannot move, I'm thinking about you.

I dare say it was just you'd had a few
and he mistook you for an easy lay.
Outside my window pane, the sky is blue.

But why did you respond? I wish I knew.
The note you left was curt, and didn't say.
I cannot move, I'm thinking about you.

Am I awake? Is all this really true?
Then who's beside me under my duvet?
Outside my window pane the sky is blue.
I cannot move, I'm thinking about you.

Shopper

I am spending my way out
of a recession. The road chokes
on delivery vans.

I used to be Just Looking Round,
I used to be How Much, and
Have You Got it in Beige.

Now I devour whole stores –
high speed spin; giant size; chunky gold;
de luxe springing. Things.

I drag them round me into a stockade.
It is dark inside; but my credit cards
are incandescent.

Soothsayer

I'm sure you will be very happy with this bra, Madam,
she said, her manicure seriously red as she tapped the till.
Of course I did not ask her how she knew.

Who is rude enough to challenge the clairvoyant,
the diagnostician, the prognosticator?
But she was right. As soon as she folded up

the lacy garment – its ticket swinging insouciantly –
and handed it across the counter
in its raspberry-pink bag, my spirits rose.

Outside, traffic parted for me like the Red Sea:
the sun appeared and gilded passers-by
who nervously returned my random smiles.

The days, the weeks, wore on in a numinous haze
of goodwill. Who knows why? Be cynical if you must:
I only record the sequence of events.

Things

Setting out from Harrods, or from
discount stores, the belongings of the nation
pass from hand to hand, disseminating
through car boot sales and burglaries,
landing up in the back rooms of Oxfam shops,
or the bric-à-brac counters at fêtes.

Neophiliacs, we restlessly pursue
a magic carpet for a dull bedroom;
a treasure from an attic, a letter
in a pocket, a trophy, a fresh view –
some dusty looking-glass
that we can step right through.

Adaptability

It sprang to life
in the airing cupboard –

shouldering the clothes aside
with its virile thrusting –

and soon burst out of the closet
into four coral ear trumpets.

Suburban insects stared in briefly
through the windows, fearing

for their sanity. Such power!
Even the stamens arched forward like gestures.

Now, the amaryllis is tendered
like ordinary tokens of civility –

the chocolates, the crimped carnations:
How nice – an amaryllis.

We are too adaptable. We grow used
to the unthinkable event.

The Idea

Standing idly at the window, she decides
to introduce her two friends, A and B
to each other. They are sure to get on.

At first they do not;
and then they do – warming
to badinage over the ratatouille.

Weeks later, someone remarks:
A and B are on holiday together.
A postcard arrives, signed by both,

funny and silly, with a view of a lake.
She stands at the window, chipping away
at the flaking paint for something to do.

Death Mask

I expected to work in privacy
but the body was laid out in a room
where solemn, portly men were drinking sherry
and whispering across the bed.
One clapped me on the shoulder:
We've heard such good reports of you, Maclaine.

I was young for so skilled a task.
Laying out my instruments
I blushed with nerves.

The head on the pillow was beaky, bewhiskered –
familiar to me from a dozen portraits.
My hands steadied a little. I took up
my spatula. As I worked, the room grew silent.

Tomorrow, someone told me, *is the lying-in-state.*

The time came to remove the mask.
I lifted the edge...and lifted
and lifted...until I saw –
with the certainty of nightmare –
that the great moustaches were tearing from the face
leaving it naked, weak, diminished.

With an oblique murmur I left the room,
made God-speed to the coast;
left the country in a packet-boat;
and fetched up here, in mining...Another brandy?

No, I never take the English papers.

Bad Timing

After his wife died
he grieved in a darkened room,
loving her at last.

A Cure for Love

I sing the love homeopathic:
it cures you before very long.
You take just a speck
of that pain-in-the-neck
and you let it dissolve on your tongue.

Your heart gains a healthy resistance:
you're done with love's visceral pain
You may miss the bliss
of that first tender kiss
but it won't strike you witless again.

Psycho-Cricket

My analyst runs in, dressed in white,
fresh from the nets
where he's been knocking up.

Un-velcroing his gloves with his teeth
he waves me to the couch.
Did you dream last night?

I give him my panic dream
of missing the last train home,
and searching for a coach instead.

His eyes glint. *This dream*
he says, *is about the English*
cricket team.

Notice the word 'train'.
We need them to train
till they drop in the crease.

He picks up a bat, takes
middle and off at the coffee table.
And then how did the dream go?

Reluctantly I mention the coach.
Of course, the coach —
archetypal team icon!

I edge in my own theories
relating to identity, inadequacy
and indigestion,

and he makes a firm sweep to leg,
clearing the mantelpiece of its clutter.
Don't hunt for obscurities, he frowns.

Taking Mrs E. to Casualty

ADMISSIONS DEPARTMENT. It didn't seem right to be grinning.
We'd brought the old lady and handed her into
their keeping. Two women with sensible
handbags, under the striplights, giggling.

Light-headedness probably – you were zonked out
from watching the polo at Chevening. I was unstrung
by the turn of events in the evening. (You nudged me:
For God's sake don't laugh, it looks so unfeeling.)

Our protégé slept in her cubicle
where we could see her. They wrote down my name
on her notes as *her next-door neighbour*. She opened an eye
and muttered the name of her cat and the nurse noted that.

The doctor was ready at last. The curtains were closing.
We tried to fall silent. It seemed like a time for musing
and wondering who would be next for the ambulance bell.
We straightened our faces and waited, cheery as hell.

Prognosis

Smith next door is sick,
poor chap. If he dies, we'll have
much more room to park.

Distance

Sooner a rich man into Heaven's eye
than I to you.

What space you have, you keep.
What time you have, you choose.

Yet once we met as if we had come close.
You held the cup and raised it to my mouth.

But that was a different story
in another part of the town.

Single Parent

Because she shares the bedroom with the baby
she undresses in the dark
and tonight her underclothes flash

and crackle in the dry air, like
miniature lightning, like
silver fireworks. It reminds her

of strobe lights, and her old crowd.
She trips and cracks her head on the bedstead
but of course must not cry out.

Our Life in Cars

Long before our first mortgage
we racketed round in that old Rolls Royce –
fifty pounds' worth of worm-holed woodwork
balding tyres and eccentricity, bought in a pub
from an itinerant Irishman.

Winding the glass partition up and down
between us was our first game; perching
on three feather pillows, I was high enough to drive.
One winter an old lady slept in it for a week
in the road outside.

But we had to part with this students' rag
of a car, grow into something safer and wiser,
with a petrol gauge and locks. The years passed soberly,
until I rode some late night taxis, and you broke out
into your Jag.

Immortality

Unwittingly, I have discovered
the secret of immortality.

But already my life is in hazard
from lobbyists and special interest groups;

stone masons, actuaries, younger sons,
environmentalists. Naturally

I have become reclusive. The grass outside
has forgotten the feel of a foot.

From the window I watch the dissolution
of my barns; the encroachment of shrubs.

Once there were paths, but now
the spotted laurels have closed their ranks:

they grow towards me, sombre as undertakers.

Blackheath

September 9th 1876

I never was in such a crush
in all my life: and just at two,
the rain came down in torrents.

The steam from our clothes
formed a heavy mist above our heads.
And still they came, thousands upon thousands.

At last the barriers gave way.
Many lost their footing in the rush
while I was carried forward by the crowd
and ended up before the speaker's stage.

When the great man arrived
there was a huge ovation.
All who had hats and lungs
employed them with a will.

He looked like one
who'd done his work about the world:
deep furrows on his face,
a few grey locks on his neck,
yet still a flashing eye.
Mrs Gladstone stayed a step behind.

For more than an hour he spoke
and from the crowd, hardly a murmur.
We drank in his words.

Russia, he said, had been our enemy
but now that she had changed her tune,
she was our friend.

At last he left us, to tremendous cheers.

The rain, which had ceased when he began,
now began as he ceased.

What a day it had been!
In our heavy, sodden clothes,
we moved away like sleepwalkers
waking to our ordinary lives.

Old Tom

He walked into the lake one night –
bricks in his pocket,
his tools neat in his cottage,
his dog shot; the last of his loaf
thrown to the birds.

The Colonel sighs with annoyance:
his grass shoots up
wild with abandon. But Tom
was tired of it all, and the lake
has taken him out of himself.

Psycho

a Victorian automaton

Whist is the game I play – but truly
I do not always win. With my dark, neat
fingers, I pick out the cards
and between games, I smoke a cigarette.
I can answer questions from the audience,
spelling out words with an alphabet.
My robes are velvet and I never move from my seat.

My age? I was two years in the making.
Maskelyne is my master, my guide, my mentor.
Here in the Egyptian Hall, the curtain has risen on me
four thousand times. I nod down from my dais
at the rapt faces. The questions they ask
recur, and time after time I give them
the certainties they are searching for.

Just Until

So I said to the Casting Director
I've got until April 10th
and she said to me

I think there's some mistake.
It's a grey-haired man we need all right
but it's only one line of dialogue.

One line! And I'd trolled right up
to Dean Street on the sodding tube.
One line! What would my agent say?

When I worked with Dickie that time
he used to tell me: It's all yours now lovey.
The sky's the limit.

Well yes. In the end I thought
I might as well. Just for a lark.
Just until something turns up.

The Agent

Interviews: try to remember
where you are. You can mention your mother –
but sparingly.

You'll be airport-to-airport in America.
Instil the eyedrops before touchdown
and tease out the fringe –

a touch of androgyny helps. I'll handle
the niche marketing and the hampers
of crisp T-shirts.

Synergy's the name of the game.
I'll always be at your back – you can be
90 per cent certain.

Thin Ice

What I'm trying to do
is to get right through to the end
without anyone noticing
(or saying to my face)
that I am an immature person who is
only pretending to be an adult.

Thresholds

Sometimes the temptation
to step over the last heartbeat
into a different world
is hard to resist.

Held in the headlights
of some profound despair
he sits tight, hangs on,
smiles when spoken to.

But round his feet he sees
cracks opening
and from their depths,
something tentacular is uncoiling.

Choir Practice

Feeling bold, she permits herself
a furtive glance into his open mouth
as she faces him, singing her heart out.

Her hymn sheet fibrillates,
agitating waves of eau de Cologne.
Her neck tenses with longing.

Once, he hung his coat over hers
on a peg in the vestry, and afterwards
her jacket smelled deliciously

of brandy and tobacco, and on its
velvet collar lay a silver hair:
portent, memento, treasured keepsake.

Mr and Mrs R and the Christmas Card List

Shall I cross them off?
It's twenty years since we last met.

Of course Mr R and I once thought
we were made for each other –

Ah, that heart-stopping moment
by the kitchen sink, when he took off

his spectacles and fiercely kissed me.
But all that lasted less than a week

and what I recall more vividly
is Mrs R's good advice:

*Always plunge your lemons in hot water
before you squeeze them.*

One more year perhaps.

Hoi!

If you are fond of love-making, try
not to be a camel in your next incarnation
for their libido depends

on massive ingestion of a small
yellow flower, which is often struck
by drought, thus posing the camel

and his cameleer many problems,
both erotic and financial. Also, camels
(if we believe the experts)

might have become extinct without humans
to assist them in their sexual congress,
lugging and positioning their awkward bodies –

which otherwise tend to overbalance –
and holding them in position during
mating with encouraging slaps

and cries of *hoi*. What is more,
foreplay in the camel
consists of foaming at the mouth.

Incubus

Yesterday
a trouble moved in on you.
and now, this morning,
it crouches on the bedpost
plain as a gargoyle.
Try to enjoy your breakfast.
Try not to notice
its claws in your neck.

Mrs Scipio's Umbrella

Buttoning himself into a clean shirt
at his bedroom window, he saw old Mrs Scipio
next door having tea in her garden
under a striped umbrella
evidently about to eat
a very elaborate piece of cake.

When he drew back his curtains in the morning,
Mrs Scipio was still there,
her head fallen sideways, the cake
half eaten, the striped umbrella
ballooning in the wind, like a sail
anxious to take off across water.

The Night He Had Thirty-Two Pints

I meant to put your roses in a jug
but right at the beginning of the shift
they brought this boy in. It was touch and go.
Another stabbing – much like all the rest.
The hangers-on were getting in the way,
drinking from cans and shouting their complaints.
Someone must have sent for the police
but we were busy pouring in the blood –
pint after pint – and most of it ran out
on swabs and landed wetly in the bin
together with his T-shirt – dyed maroon
and scissored up through LAY ONE ON FOR ME.
He had two pints for each year of his life.
The clerk rang up his mother and she came
half wild – we heard her shouting at the desk.
Later, I saw her sitting on a bench
subdued and shaking, chattering her teeth
against a mug of tea. Her eldest son
lay like a bone, a conduit, a test
of what we could achieve. At half past three
we sent him up to Wilkins in T 5.

Despite the rush, the night dragged on for years.

We didn't win...
                    sorry about the flowers.

The Optimist

My father, in his last hospital bed
on the eve of a critical operation,
negotiated to buy from another patient
an electric razor, slightly faulty.
My mother, realist to the end
discouraged this purchase.

They argued the pros and cons
until the porter came with the trolley.
It was something to talk about
at that time, which is so awkward –
awkward and sad as waiting for a lover
to be carried away, waving, in a train.

Harriet

The cat drowses in an ambush of flowers;
each tree sits in its dish of shadow
against the faultless blue.

The world and his wife
are lazing away the hours, in retreat
until the resurrection of teatime.

Two days old, you lie
provisionally silent, waiting for night to cue
your rich, nocturnal, operatic life.

Pastoral

He pushes the pram, straight-armed,
away from the scrap yard, over the lumpy field
towards the further edge, where the M 25
bites into the boundary. His grandson
bounces, stoical and woolly-hatted.

He tries to map out the place
where he picknicked fifty years ago
with Hazel Jones. Fish paste sandwiches
and Tizer, warm from dusty saddlebags.
She stung her leg and he spat on it for her.

He imagines her rising in front of him
out of a mist, her brown hair swinging –
like a shampoo commercial. But God grant
he never meets her in the flesh – to compare
their hip joints, their grandchildren's teeth.

Sunday Lunchtime

The whirlpools of the launderette
do not recognise the Sabbath,

so the air in Worple Street
smells of soapsuds and roast beef.

The Church of Healing is silent
with endeavour – and the Oddfellows

have gathered in their Hall –
now they'll be there till evening.

Mr Patel leans on his counter
and reads about HEAVEN ON EARTH –

A celestial city discovered by *Sunday Sport*
as a change from sex. In the street

Concorde glides across car windows,
noisy as hell, but tiny as a paper dart.

The Star and the Birds

In the New Year, it starts with
a star. They point to it on her X-ray –
white, fragile, filamented,
sinister as a footstep in a dark alley.

She packs a bag, reads her horoscope.
On the ward the trolleys come and go
freighted with figures,
white-capped, whey-faced, dopey.

Taking his coarse pen (*Excuse me*)
the houseman draws an arrow
on her breast. It points to her heart
like some ironic early Valentine.

The ceiling of the anaesthetic room
is painted – its theme is zoological.
She watches the tropical birds
blur in a mêlée of bright wings.

At home her kitchen,
under its fine frost of dust,
listens to the answering machine
whirring and parroting.

Rust

It's important to scrape off
all the flakes first: even I know that.
Then the rust solution must be scrunched in
with steel wool, round the wing mirror,
where the surface is abraded.
Fine sun and wind help the drying.
Shoo off the cabbage whites, mating
dangerously near the chemicals
and stand aside for the bearded man
with his pram full of leaflets on carpet cleaning
which he is letterboxing with audible clickings
of his sparse teeth. The road is emptyish,
it being August: just Peggy in overalls
painting her front door yellow, and Wayne
carting in the giant prawns for his Sunday barbecue.
My reflection in the windscreen looks grave
but I am perilously happy as I lean on the bonnet
under the blue sky, waiting for the moment
when I can start touching in the mulberry red paint.

Here Today

Whether to get the cheaper
or the more expensive stair-carpet

is the problem. The salesman asks me:
Are you the only person living in your house?

What next? Must I offer up my age,
state of health, genetic profile?

I point to the cheaper, shorter-life carpet.
Annoyingly he nods in agreement.

Tabula Rasa

At eighty, he set himself the task
of repainting his rooms. He worked slowly,
wheezing up and down the folding steps.

He chose the blue of his old cricket club tie;
the half-recollected gold of his wife's hair
when they first met in Rawalpindi;

and an ash-grey, which brought to mind
his son's death — that dark year
of hope and despair

In the evenings he was meticulous
with his white spirit, laying out the brushes,
battening down the lids of the tins.

Nine days after finishing, he keeled forward
over *The Times*, and closed his eyes
on a final view of his hearthrug.

Young couples came to view the property:
Perfect. We'll only need to give the place
a couple of coats of brilliant white.

Last Haiku

No, wait a minute,
I can't be old already:
I'm just about to